Dedication

To Noah Habib — A truly amazing and empowering friend whose 'special' gifts far exceed his 'special' needs that he is too often labeled by.

Keep Rocking Noah!

WALLY THE WAVE!

A Salty Story of Social Inclusion in the spirit of 'Oneness'

...but as Wally soon discovers, a 'oneness' far from 'Sameness!'

Written by: Rev Ryan Althaus

...with the wisdom, spiritual, inspirational, & artistic assistance of the one & only Noah Habib! Watch @ https://youtu.be/J8jendfl8hs

"I am conscious of a soul-sense
that lifts me above the narrow,
cramping circumstances of my life.
My physical limitations are forgotten-
my world lies upward, the length and
the breadth and the sweep of
the heavens are mine!"

— Helen Keller, The Story of My Life

"We learn more (grow more) through an hour of play
than a lifetime of conversation"   -Plato

The gifts we bear are diverse,
but each flows from one source;
we bear one spirit.
1 Cor 12:4

"Today you are you... that is truer than true.
There is no one alive who is Youer than YOU!"
-Dr. Suess

People who are homeless
are not social inadaquates,
they are people without houses.
-Sheila McKechnie

"UNBANTU! I AM ME
BECAUSE YOU ARE YOU!"
-DESMOND TUTU

"True nobility is not found through
our superiority to our fellow man,
but our superiority to our former
selves."
-Ernest Hemingway

"A human being is part of the whole,
called by us 'universe,' (or Wally the Wave's ocean!)
a part limited in time and space. He experiences himself,
his thoughts and feelings, as something separate
from the rest-a kind of optical delusion of consciousness.
This delusion is a kind of prison for us, restricting
us to our personal desires and to affection for a few persons
nearest to us. Our task must be to free ourselves from this
prison by widening our circle of compassion to embrace all
living creatures and the whole of nature in its beauty."
— Albert Einstein, 1921

"Re-Creation is possible
through RECreation"
-Ryan Althaus

"Thousands of candles can be lighted from a single
candle, and the life of the candle will not be shortened.
Happiness never decreases by being shared."   -Buddah

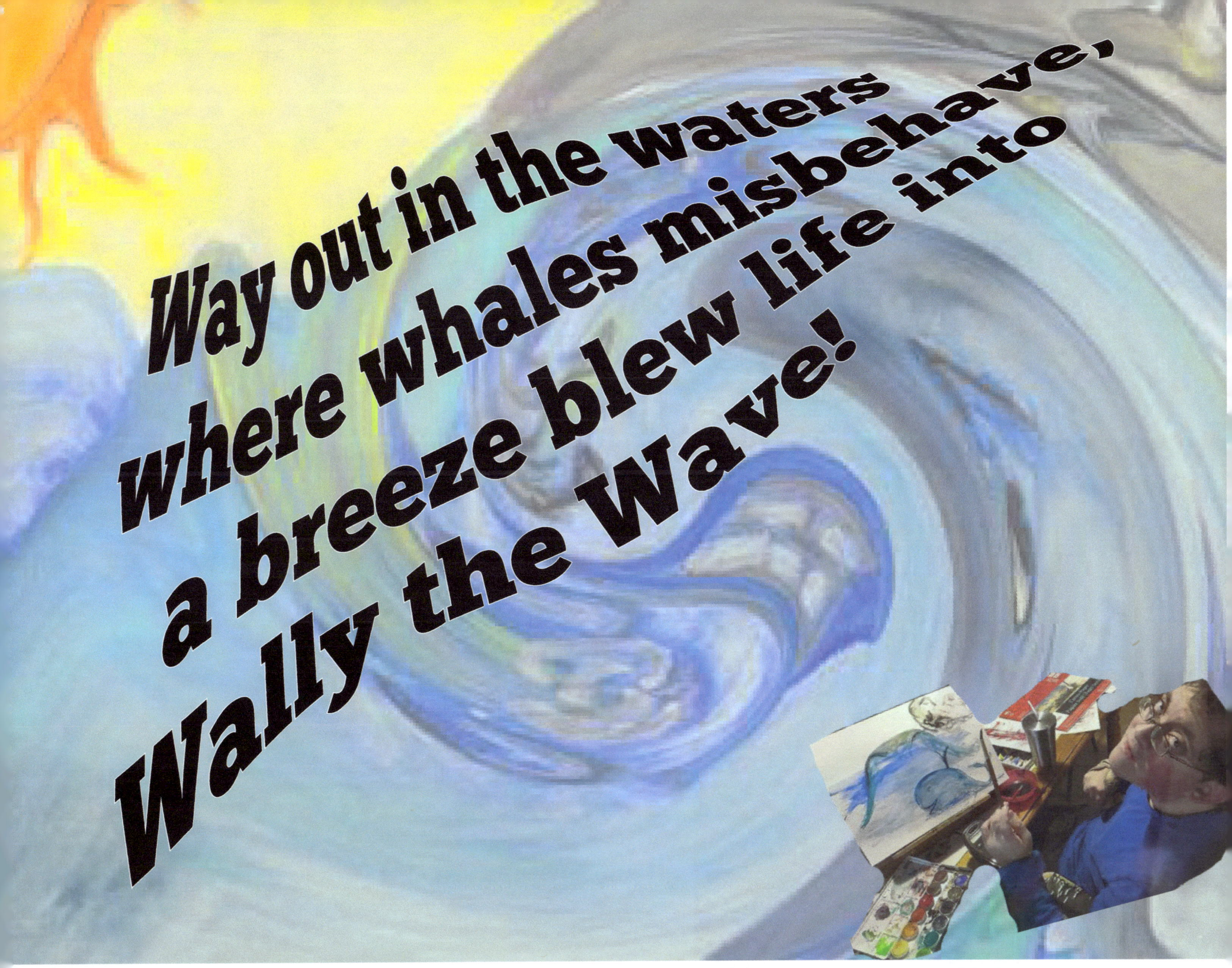

Way out in the waters
where whales misbehave,
a breeze blew life into
Wally the Wave!

while brightly reflecting
sun, star, and moon

Wally wandered night &
day whistling tropical tunes.

He delighted the dolphins who dove in his wake and plundered poor pirates whose treasure he'd take.

Squid, Shark, and Seahorse swam all around...

...colorful coral caves where strings of seaweed abound.

Under his belly
a wondrous wet world
swirled with life...

...full of frolicking fish of
every color, size, & strife.

Traveling westward Wally widened in the wind, passing long-lost islands ancient sailors had pinned.

Wally winced when he watched a wave break on the shore, and he trembled with fear at the sound of its roar!

Wally's eyes cringed closed as whitewater swirled on his head, and someone yelled 'wipeout' at a bodacious body-surfer named Fred.

An explosion of water sent shells soaring into the sky... ...but a rather strange sound took the place of Wally's final cry.

Wally's eyes slowly opened to a magnificent surprise. A new world surrounded him as bright as the sunrise!

"If only there was a way of telling people that they are all walking around shining like the sun."
~ Thomas Merton

...but now he was more than a mere wave, he was part of an ocean!

One with the water and part of a larger whole...

Before just a weak wall of water, Wally was now part of the tide's unified roll!

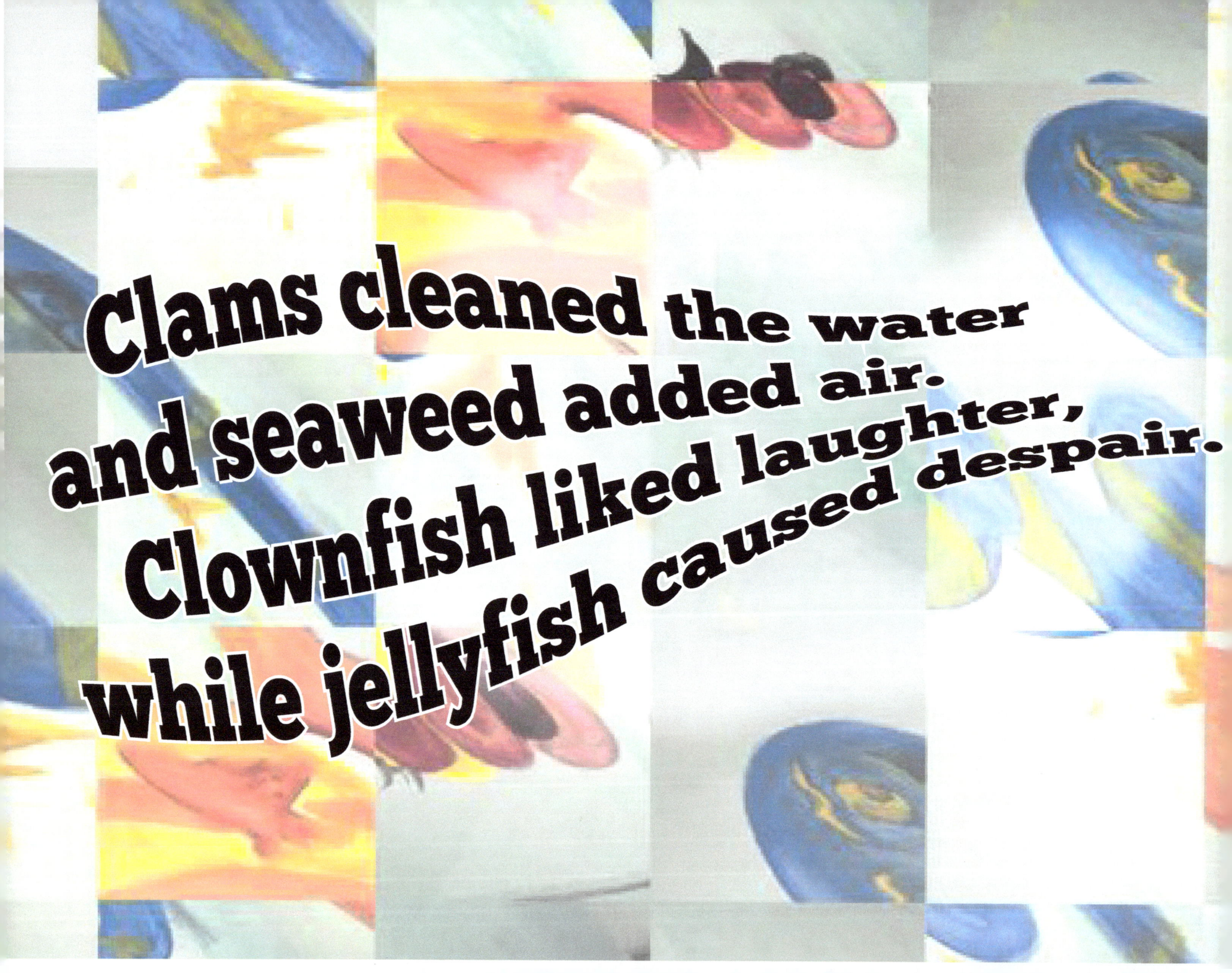

Clams cleaned the water
and seaweed added air.
Clownfish liked laughter,
while jellyfish caused despair.

So always remember
that you are more than
a wandering wave.
You are part of an ocean
so stand tall, mighty,
and brave!

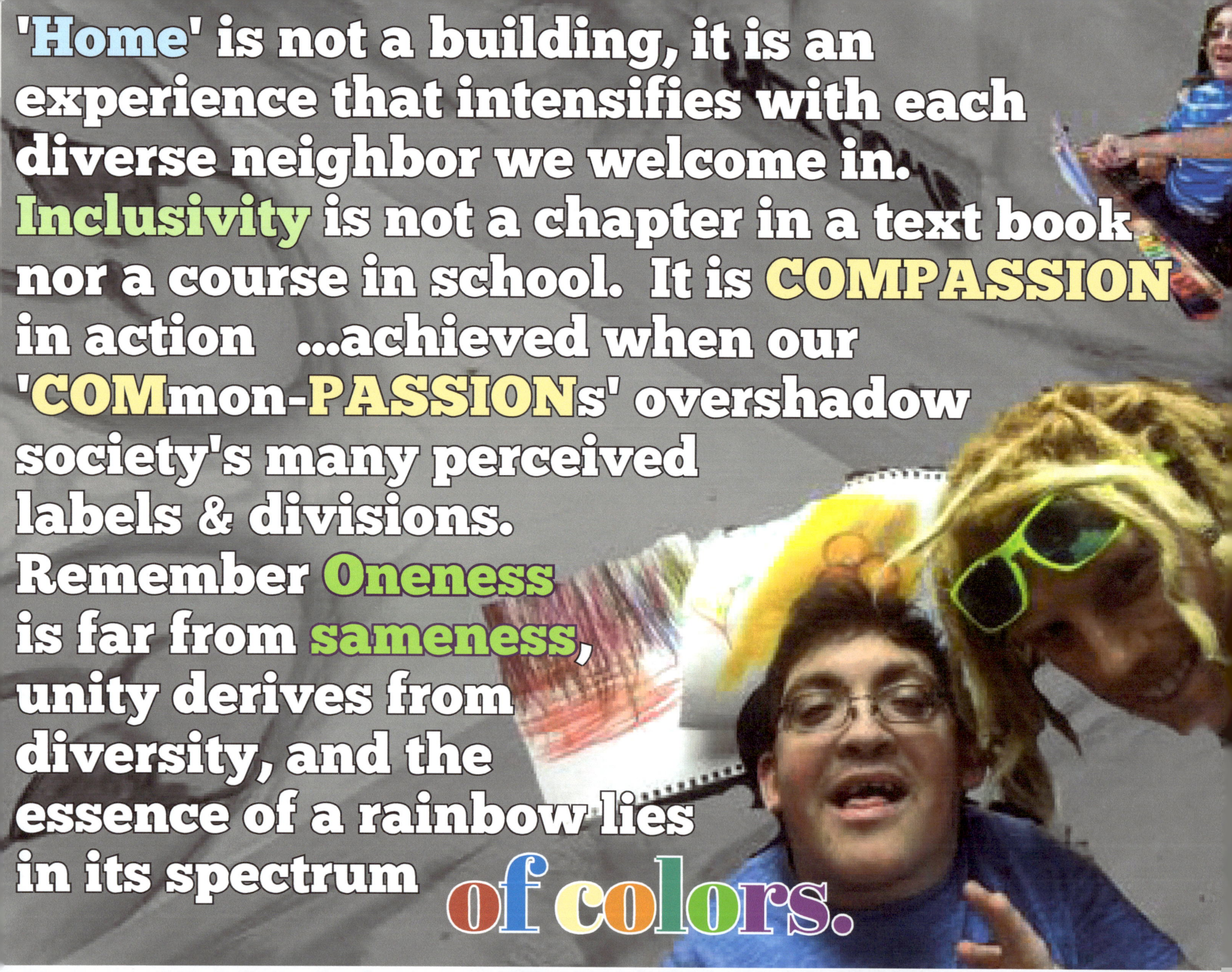

'Home' is not a building, it is an experience that intensifies with each diverse neighbor we welcome in. Inclusivity is not a chapter in a text book nor a course in school. It is COMPASSION in action ...achieved when our 'COMmon-PASSIONs' overshadow society's many perceived labels & divisions. Remember Oneness is far from sameness, unity derives from diversity, and the essence of a rainbow lies in its spectrum of colors.

A Wee Chapter for the 'Grown-ups' to Enhance your Experience with Wally:

The tale of Wally's Wanderings to follow was inspired by the Persian poet and Sufi mystic, Rumi's, poem, *A Garden Beyond Paradise* and I hope you take time to read the poem concluding this little introduction, and in doing so, allow yourself to get lost in your own 'wanderings' while exploring what 'oneness' means in your own life as well as the lives of your family, friends, and neighbors. The term "*Mystic*" may sound a little 'strange.' A little 'weird.' However, despite any questions, thoughts, or images the term may stir up, 'mystics' are simply individuals who place more value on 'experience' than 'word.' After-all, 'words' are but second-hand descriptions of experiences…and the best experiences are those that transcend description! By embracing the creative, inclusive, and curious spirit of children - *their mystical and magical nature* - the wise and passionate voice of Rumi and his mystic mob remain prevalent voices in a variety of literary, faith, and philosophical schools throughout the ages. Speaking of ages, when it comes to '*getting lost*' in experience and imagination, what better teacher, rabbi, prophet, or philosopher than the nearest curious kiddo? *And you don't even need your own!* Borrow a neighbor's youngster (who knows, you may even get a few dollars for babysitting) and soak up their contagious mystic spirit! Just make sure to ask first as the difference between 'babysitting' and 'kidnapping' could definitely dampen your day!

Wally's story is the first in a series of writings that seek to explore diverse 'difficult' topics such as anger, depression, interfaith relations, and so forth alongside those wise sages we deem 'children.' By engaging our youth in open and deliberate discussions around difficult social, ethical, and faith topics during the formative years of childhood can cultivate a deeper sense of compassion, acceptance, and equality that provokes our communal evolution towards a more holistic and just worldview for generations to come. That said, us 'grown-ups' have just as much to gain from the unbiased perspectives, open minds, and hopeful hearts of our youth! So dive into the ocean of inclusivity with the nearest kiddo-companion and wander with Wally while watching the magical twinkle in their eyes! As you do, soak up a bit of their unadulterated acceptance and innocence in hopes of healing some of your own wounds, broadening your own vision, and bridging divisions present in your own community as you travel the sacred seas together!

Wally's wisdom in our own lives and community...

Everyday our children encounter a variety of mis-'labeled,' mis-perceived, or adversely stereotyped populations. Our society categorizes and divides individuals based on their economic status, race, religion, abilities/disabilities, ethnicity, age, et cetera. These learned biases, often intertwined with emotions of anger, fear, or misperception, are easily and often unintentionally passed on to the open ears, minds, and hearts of our youth. In the story to follow, *Wally the Wave* discovers the essence of -*not the structure of*-'home' amidst a diverse ocean community as he transitions from a wave on top of, to a unique and essential component of, one unified sea. Wally's 'homecoming' serves as a parable for all ages -*and species of the air, earth and ocean*- reminding us that we are not unified **despite of,** but **because of,** our differences! An awakening to the notion that 'oneness' is far from **'sameness!'**

By utilizing relevant, deliberate, and organic shared experiences -intentional, playful, purposeful, and dignified interactions with diverse neighbors- as safe spaces for formative interaction and storytelling, we are able to transcend the labels, or 'words,' that fuel sociologically imposed biases and prejudice. Children are uniquely gifted in one particular '*shared experience…*' That which we refer to as '**PLAY!**' The laughter-filled, '*commonly-unifying,*' sounds of **'play'** provide a foundation for the cultivation of authentic '**comm-unity**' with those different than 'us.' It is my hope that we strive to keep our children blind to, but not ignorant of, the segregating and stigmatizing labels of society so they may continue to see the world through unbiased eyes as they grow… Eyes open wide to the many beautiful -and *beautifully complementary*-hues of one unified rainbow… Eyes open to the brilliant colors reflected by Wally and many unique and playful waves that texturize one magnificent ocean!

Key thoughts/questions to guide you and your child's reading experience:

◆ What do the words 'community, companion, and compassion' have in common? The prefix '**com-**' or '**common**!' Each word stresses our interconnectedness and expresses our '**common**-alities' in different ways:

◆"**Community-** " That '*welcoming home*' to which Wally wanders! Holistic 'community' is rooted in our '*common-unities.*' Be it a sporting event, a club, volunteering or working together… sharing in a common experience serves as a 'common-unifier' that allows those things that bring us together to overshadow superficial labels and misperceptions that divide. What 'common-unities' are relevant or present in your life and community? How can they be used to welcome in new diverse neighbors of populations your family may be disconnected from or curious about?

◆**Compassion**- '*Common-passion*!' We may not like, get along with, or understand everyone we meet. Thats okay. Natural even! However, by sharing a '*common-passion*' (a common experience/feeling/emotion) we may feel and share compassion towards the unique situations of diverse neighbors. Compassion is different than sympathy. Compassion is about providing a 'hand up, not a 'hand out.' It is a humanizing experience that dignifies, empowers, and heals both parties. This view of compassion may best be expressed in the age-old adage of 'walking a mile in another's shoes.' What shoes could your family try on which would expand your appreciation, understanding, and acceptance of new friends?

◆**Companionship**- 'Common-Panion.' 'Panion' is latin for 'Bread,' but it depicts much more than food and addresses a hunger much louder than a growing tummy. *Companionship* is where the notion of 'communion,' *the breaking of bread together,* is derived. We all share a 'common' indiscriminate hunger for companionship… an insatiable yearning for acceptance! Reflect with your child on how sharing a meal with someone new fills both soul and belly. Try inviting a homeless friend to lunch instead of dropping a dollar in a hat the next time you're meandering down the street and experience how it fills your and their soul with the fruits of companionship! After-all, the most painful part of being 'homeless,' 'disabled,' or 'different' is often not being without house or certain ability, but the social implications of being stereotyped by these things enact. We all crave acceptance and purpose, but the labels we've been ascribed can infringe on our ability to find it. Companionship starts with acknowledging one another by name, not number… by seeing a person, not a perception! It is as simple as offering a warm greeting to a neighbor in need. An authentic smile is beautifully free, it is far from cheap, so share smiles abundantly throughout your day and feed off those you receive in return!

◆ **What groups/individuals are on the fringes of your neighborhood?** We live in a divided society. Some of these divisions are natural and some are learned. Regardless of where these divisions were derived, **how about exploring them instead of ignoring them**! What groups cause you discomfort? Which invoke curiosity? Confusion? Anger? Discomfort? Openly discuss how these feelings, various perceptions, and stereotypes can keep 'them' from being equal members of 'our' community. Then brainstorm with your child relevant ways that your family might engage new friends in relationships of mutual growth.

◆ '**Homeless**?' Children see a variety of 'house-less' neighbors daily. These friends are burdened by stereotypical notions/labels such as addict, dirty, crazy, lazy, and so forth. Sometimes these 'words' are true, but more often not… and in any case, they are not intrinsically connected to one's housing situation. It is easy to reiterate negative labels through our daily conversations and comments without realizing the messages we are sending to the open ears of our youth! Teach your children how to share hope and acceptance with those in need through positive speech that emphases the value, potential, and uniqueness of everyone that you pass by on the street. Despite our best of intentions, traditional outreach efforts such as mass meals or collections of food/clothing can enhance labels of inadequacy via further dividing 'us' and 'them.' Help your child see all individuals as unique people with names and value so that they do not become mere numbers or recipients of superficial resources by reiterating ways of which we all serve each-other… not our serving 'the other.' As Hemingway eloquently wrote, *"True nobility is not found through our superiority to our fellow man, but through our superiority to our former selves."*

◆ '**Disabled**?' Rates of autism, cerebral palsy, depression/anxiety and so on are on the rise and in the news. Children are exposed to a variety of unique friends in school and at play daily. This book was co-illustrated by a special friend of mine, Noah, who exemplifies a population too often defined by their special 'needs,' not their special gifts. It can be difficult for these 'special' neighbors to find acceptance because we do not know how to treat them nor do we fully understand their situation. By freeing ourselves from stigmas we start to grow comfortable interacting with special needs neighbors and soon develop relationships that allow these friends to share about (even joke about) their uniqueness. Do not let a fear of offending or misunderstanding another ever stand in the way of a beautifully fulfilling friendship! Lift up one another's **gifts**, not their **needs**!

◆ **LGBTQ-** The rainbow representatives! We are making waves (pun intended) in the field of sexual orientation/identification through the many pride parades brightening city streets around the county; however, we have a ways yet to go. Next time you look at a rainbow in the sky alongside your children notice how the colors are not distinctly divided, but blend with one another in a beautiful skyward watercolor masterpiece! Allow the L's, G's, B's, T's and Q's to follow suit so that our many colors serve to complement, not contrast, one another! The paintings Noah and I used for this work were done in watercolor for a reason. Color lines in watercolor are messy, blended, and beautiful... So it should be with our world! Ditch the distinctions and scribble outside the lines!

◆ **Race/ethnicity-** (refugee) This is another hot issue in modern culture; however, we are all refugees if we travel our ancestral roots deeply enough. The racial or ethnic roots we bear should provide foundations, not limitations, on which the dreams, purpose, passions, and potential of all may blossom. Live a borderless life, ignorant to the fear and hatred which fuels deportation, discrimination, and division! Disregard any personal metaphoric or literal borders and hopefully our country will follow suite!

◆ **Political/Religious**... In a time of which 'political correctness' provides a prime example of oxymoron and political/religious labels of democrat or republican, conservative or liberal, evangelical or progressive, and the like fuel heated ('moronic') newscasts and radio ramblings, we all may benefit from a quick reflection on political and faith affiliations. We are all are entitled our own views, but with that we are also responsible for evaluating each circumstance with open minds and ears. We are responsible to think for ourselves, not to blindly accept the views of others based on our or 'their' social, political, or religious affiliations. For its been said that 'thinking independently together' is the difference between responding and reacting and it creates a safe space for all to stay true to their morals, values, and beliefs in our true pursuit of 'life, liberty, and **happiness!'**

All that said, we all have preferences based on a variety of mentioned and unmentioned factors, affiliations, experiences, etc... thats Normal! Just remember:

...**Preference** occurs when we see and respect all the choices, but prefer, or are more comfortable with, one over the other. For 'preference' to be healthy, it requires dialogue and open-mindedness, In this sense it can actually allow our diversity to foster a unifying mutual evolution. Its a natural occurrence that needs to be acknowledged, and as long as it is not ignored, it can even be helpful.

...**Prejudice** occurs when we hide or ignore preference. It thrives when we choose one way or accept one label without opening ourselves to learn from or grow alongside the other. It is the root of conformity and is founded on fear, insecurity, and a lack of communication which starts when our 'preferences' are ignored.

...**Racism** occurs when our resentments and prejudices (our fears) are suppressed and turn to hatred. It is the belief that the only way to be ourselves lies in belittling or discriminating our neighbor. Racism occurs when suppressed preference and prejudice mix with personal insecurities and is only overcome through dialogue.

Noah, Wally, and a whole lot of FUN! The creation of Wally the Wave!

Our children are unique in their ability to see beyond labels... to 'not judge a book by its cover' nor a person by their color. However, they are not alone! Leading up to this book's composition I have been blessed to work directly alongside three distinct populations. Each unique in their situation, but united by a common thread of social misperception and a common yearning for acceptance and purpose. Each of these populations (special needs, houseless, and recovery) are repeatedly limited by sociological labels ('disabled, homeless, addict') and each of these 'labels' creates a barrier between 'them' and 'us' restricting their ability to lead purposeful, fulfilling, and dignified lives. Moreover, these labels prevent us '*normal*' folk from receiving the abundant gifts of wisdom and companionship of very 'special' neighbors.

In the spirit of playfulness and diverse companionship all of the pictures filling the following pages were painted with two hands! Not my right and left -ambidexterity is not a talent of mine- but my own hand intertwined with the hand of Noah. At age 22, Noah indeed offers more 'special gifts' than 'special needs' through his **'ability'** to see the world with the unbiased and unadulterated love, acceptance, and vision of a child. He is ***uniquely-'able'*** to **'dis'**-regard differences so to lose himself in the ***experience*** of companionship, compassion, and community. His ***'unique-abilities'*** are only hindered by his being labeled '***dis-abled;*** however, that doesn't limit his lyrical laughter, dim his radiant shine, or shut his open arms and heart.

Noah has advanced cerebral palsy, a neurological disorder affecting motor control functions of the brain that cause paralysis and inhibit his ability for vocal speech. However, Noah is famous in Santa Cruz for his amazing hugs, 'back-scratches,' animated interactions, art work, and sense of adventure! I've learned and grown so much in the several months that it took to create these images alongside of Noah. It has been a slow process for sure, but another **unique-ability** of Noah lies in his ability to step outside of the fast-paced, stressed, and worldly schedules of society and into the present. The process has taught me to leave my cell phone, watch, and expectations at home and lose myself in the moment. Not an easy thing to do! In greek their are two words for time, **chronos** (moments on a watch) and **cairos** ('moments' of significance in our lives.) The word for 'happy' (ma-'cairos') is just that, losing ourselves to worldly restrictions of quantified time and divisive label so to open our lives to the joys of eternity. For as Ludwig Witgenstien wrote, "*Eternity is given to those who live in the present.*"

Noah and I have been using watercolor paints for this project which offer their own unique metaphor. **Watercolors are about BLENDING** and **MESSINESS!** Instead of distinct lines (*expectations, perceptions, schedules, etc,*) watercolors call on the artist (*we are all artists*) to 'go with the flow.' You cannot be afraid to paint outside the lines because each color/image requires a messy mixture of paints, strokes, and imagination. Furthermore, watercolors represent the social inclusivity of which we strive! Watercolors may be the secret to allow the *l, b, t, q's to* blend alongside of purples of the blue democrats and red republicans, which further blur lines separating house-less & housed; CEO & janitor; young & old; Jew, Christian, & Muslim; male & female, male turned female, female turned male and so on as we unite to create an ocean of hues far beyond 'blue.'

Each image to follow has been done in many stages… WATCH THE PROCESS BY VISITING
https://youtu.be/J8jendfI8hs

◆ Noah and I start each session by reading Wally's adventure for the day and brainstorming just what images the words inspire and how we could put them on paper! Noah's animated responses to a series of questions and ideas guide our transformation of the blank page in front of us (you will see this fun dialogue in the video!)

◆ Once we decide what we'd like to see on the page (**not what we expect to see**) we practice various movements on scrap paper so to learn the various hand motions required for each unique shape (ie: curves of Wally, horizontal lines for horizons, circles for suns, etc.) Creating the shapes of our images is a team effort where I supplement Noah's restricted hand movements by moving the paper under him as he completes each stroke. For example, a circle image requires a full rotation of the paper as Noah paints with an arc stroke.

◆ Once we have our images in mind and practiced we pick our base colors and get messy mixing up our pallets! We start with lighter background colors, Noah and I both love the sloppiness of the background, then dive in with the increasingly distinct shapes of the foreground.

◆ The use of watercolors allows us to blend and play with colors as we go until they form into images that we are satisfied with …and Noah is very good at letting me know when he is done! The process is full of many breaks, laughs, and 'distractions' as every few strokes of the brush requires a period of rest and often a sip of water and snack. It has been great for my type 'A,' result driven personality, to learn to rest, relax, and giggle! I've had to accept that there are days when a three hour art session may yield nothing more than a blurred blotch of blues on a single page; however, when I do, it becomes quickly evident that those three hours alongside my friend Noah are more valuable than any Picasso or da Vinci!

◆ After Noah is satisfied with each page I go back and work through smaller details such as facial features and textures while being careful not to manipulate any of the strokes and authentic messiness of our shared work. When you look at the pictures to follow you will be able to see the layers of our work and the variety of strokes that compose each image. Hopefully you will be able to get lost in the moment as much as Noah and I did as you stare into the depths of each picture! I've found that going back to add detail and blend lines in the pictures has provided a beautiful chance to get lost in the emotions and purity of the creation process. By diving back into each picture, I'm able to transcend into that inexplicable experience of creating it with Noah and relive the emotions and joy our time together. Hopefully you get lost in the pictures as well… and if you need help just gaze into the eyes of your child as you read together!

A Garden Beyond Paradise
by Rumi

In his poem, **A Garden Paradise,** Rumi provides two unique metaphors of 'oneness,' the ocean and the garden. Both are images prevalent throughout ancient writings from a variety of faith traditions and cultures who trace our 'human being-ness' (human is latin for 'humus' or dirt) back to the Garden. We see an example of this when exploring the word 'Earth,' or '*Adameh*,' which in the Hebrew language of biblical creation serves as the derivative of the name 'Adam' or the first of creation. Simply said, when we garden together, dig into the unified '*adamah*' of which we were all created, we harvest a variety of literal and metaphorical 'fruits of the soil' which open doors, touch hearts and fill stomachs in the healing experience of '*Companionship!*'

Similarly, the ocean has provided a timeless source of healing and place of rebirth and play for all those surfers, sailors, and scuba divers. A place which emphasizes the '*Sweaty Sheep*' motto of '*Re-Creation through Recreation*!' Much like the garden, the sea provides a key source of nutrition… another metaphorical and literal common-panion to root our companionship and community out of. As you read the following words from Rumi, allow the poetic imagery to carry you away. Allow it to stir up dreams and visions of euphoric ocean sunsets, 'harvest fields of golden grain,' robust strawberry patches, and colorful coral reefs as you become '*not a droplet in an ocean, but an ocean in a droplet.*' Wander on!

Everything you see has its roots
in the unseen world.
The forms may change,
yet the essence remains the same.

Every wondrous sight will vanish,
every sweet word will fade.
But do not be disheartened,
The Source they come from is eternal--
growing, branching out,
giving new life and new joy.

Why do you weep?--
That Source is within you,
and this whole world
is springing up from it.

The Source is full,
its waters are ever-flowing;
Do not grieve,
drink your fill!
Don't think it will ever run dry--
This is the endless Ocean!

From the moment you came into this world,
a ladder was placed in front of you
that you might transcend it.

From earth, you became plant,
from plant you became animal.
Afterwards you became a human being,
endowed with knowledge, intellect and faith.

Behold the body, born of dust--
how perfect it has become!

Why should you fear its end?
When were you ever made less by dying?

When you pass beyond this human form,
no doubt you will become an angel
and soar through the heavens!

But don't stop there.
Even heavenly bodies grow old.

Pass again from the heavenly realm
and plunge into the ocean of Consciousness.
Let the drop of water that is you
become a hundred mighty seas.

But do not think that the drop alone
becomes the Ocean--
the Ocean, too, becomes the drop!

Sweaty Sheep is a movement calling us to engage in deliberative & interactive journeys, or *'wanderings,'* utilizing recreation as a means of breaking down sociological, economic, situational, cultural & faith divisions. In less words, we strive to promote the 'POWER OF PLAY' in the cultivation a more cohesive & FUN community! Stay up to date with new books, fun ideas, events, and all our playful pursuits at **www.sweatysheep.com** & come surf, sail, garden, pray and PLAY with us in Santa Cruz California anytime! Sweaty Sheep is a socially inclusive initiative that values the intrinsic potential, 'special gifts' and unique beauty of all faith, cultural, ethnic, and social affiliations. We don't do black & white too well! Thus we've been deemed the 'Rainbow Sheep!' A wandering flock, not afraid to question, doubt, explore, risk and make new friends (like you!) So wander with us!

About the Author:

Ryan, known in Santa Cruz as "the Pastor of Play," has spent the past several decades working intensively alongside various socially misperceived populations. His undergraduate work in english education and theology lead to a master's degree in Divinity with a focus on world religious philosophy. His 'playful pursuits' with several interfaith and nonprofit networks have helped to reveal the variety of faith, economic, and social barriers that divide the community. This inspired his pursuit of a second master's in nonprofit business with the goal of creating a grassroots organization focused on unifying, sharing, and celebrating the diversity of creation across faith, goverment, nonprofit, business, and social communities. This passion for playfulness and community now reverberates in "Sweaty Sheep's" motto, "Re-Creation through RECreation," and at any given time you'll likely find Ryan & his k-9 companion on/in the ocean, mountains, or garden. Though an ordained Presbyterian Minister, Ryan strives to promote the wisdom of ALL faith traditions, the unique story of ALL neighbors, and the intrinsic value of ALL creation in our co-evolution towards a healthier, holistic, and intentional community. As he eloquently states, 'We are each created by (and are part of) an un-comprehensible & un-nameable beauty. Regardless of what words or labels we use, we only ever experience creator through creation. Thus it is through our unbiased, unadulterated, and unrestrained love & diverse interactions with one another that we may taste true beauty. Thus its time to shut this book and go be beautiful, make new friends, & celebrate the awesomely divine world surrounding you!

www.ingramcontent.com/pod-product-compliance
Lightning Source LLC
Chambersburg PA
CBHW040820120626

46551CB00005B/611